DISCOVER "THE STAR-SPANGLED BANNER"

A Tribute to Our Nation

Cherry Lake Press

Published in the United States of America by Cherry Lake Publishing
Ann Arbor, Michigan
www.cherrylakepublishing.com

Reading Adviser: Beth Walker Gambro, MS, Ed., Reading Consultant, Yorkville, IL

Photo Credits: © Studio Basel Gallery/Shutterstock, cover, title page; Prints and Photographs Division/Library of Congress, 5; John Bower/Prints and Photographs Division/Library of Congress, 7; Smithsonian Institution Archives, 8; SrA Beaux Hebert/DVIDS/Public Domain, 9; William Congreve, Public domain, via Wikimedia Commons, 10; Courtesy of the Maryland Center for History and Culture, 11; © coronado/Shutterstock, 12; © Miblu/Shutterstock, 14; © flashbacknyc/Shutterstock, 15; © Christopher Mazmanian/Shutterstock; National Park Service, CC BY 2.0 via Wikimedia Commons, 17; Maryland National Guard/Public Domain, 18; NASA/ Apollo 11, Public domain, via Wikimedia Commons, 20; © Jacob Lund/Shutterstock, 21

Cherry Lake Press is an imprint of Cherry Lake Publishing Group

Library of Congress Cataloging-in-Publication Data has been filed and is available at catalog.loc.gov.

Cherry Lake Publishing Group would like to acknowledge the work of the Partnership for 21st Century Learning, a Network of Battelle for Kids. Please visit Battelle for Kids online for more information.

Printed in the United States of America

Note from Publisher: Websites change regularly, and their future contents are outside of our control. Supervise children when conducting any recommended online searches for extended learning opportunities.

TABLE OF CONTENTS

INTRODUCTION

The year was 1814. The War of 1812 raged on. Francis Scott Key and John Skinner were on a British warship outside of Baltimore, Maryland. They were there to **negotiate** the release of William Beanes, an American doctor the British had captured. Negotiations went well, but something was going on.

The British were about to attack Baltimore. Key, Skinner, and Beanes were not allowed to leave and warn American troops. British **detained** them for a week. Key gazed across the water at Fort McHenry. He watched the American flag flying high over the fort. He feared he would see the British flag there after the battle.

Early in the morning on September 13, the British attacked. They rained 1,500 cannonballs, shells, and rockets down on the fort. But the fort stood strong. The attack failed.

The next morning, in the early light of dawn, Francis Scott Key's chest filled with pride as he spotted the American flag waving through the smoke across the water. He pulled a letter from his pocket and began writing the poem "Defense of Fort McHenry" on the back. That poem soon became what we know as "The Star-Spangled Banner."

"THE STAR-SPANGLED BANNER"

The song "The Star-Spangled Banner" became a popular patriotic song, but it was over 100 years before it became the national anthem.

O say can you see,
by the dawn's early light,

★ **FAST FACTS** The **siege** on Fort McHenry lasted for 27 hours in heavy rain. The waters around Fort McHenry were too shallow for large warships. Bomber ships carried out the attack.

What so proudly we hail'd at the twilight's last gleaming,

★ **FAST FACTS** Fort McHenry had a large **garrison** flag as well as a smaller storm flag. Storm flags were flown during heavy weather. When the sun set on September 13, 1814, the storm flag flew over Fort McHenry.

Whose broad stripes and bright stars through the perilous fight

★ **FAST FACTS** Fort McHenry's garrison flag was enormous. It was 30 feet (9.1 meters) by 42 ft (12.8 m). Major George Armistead wanted "a flag so large that the British will have no difficulty seeing it from a distance." That was the flag Key saw after the battle.

O'er the ramparts we watch'd were so gallantly streaming?

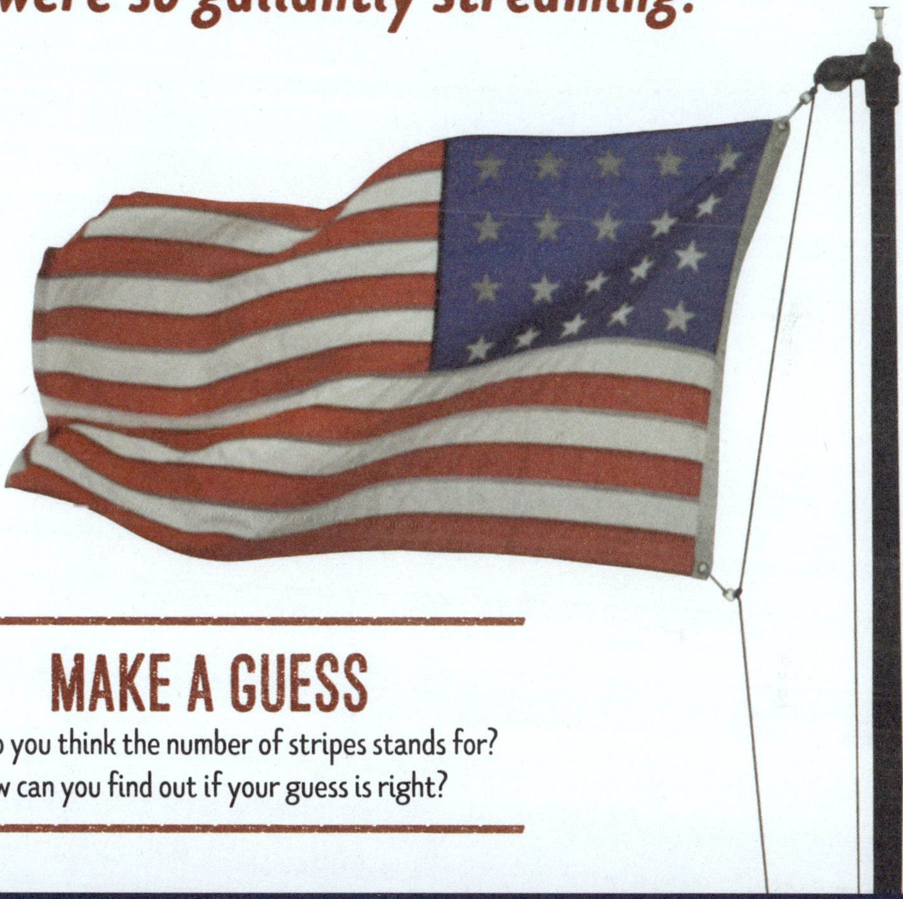

MAKE A GUESS

What do you think the number of stripes stands for?
How can you find out if your guess is right?

★ **FAST FACTS** The 1814 flag of the United States had 15 stars and 15 stripes. An act passed in 1818 changed the number of stripes on the flag to 13. The act also said a star would be added on July 4th for any new states.

And the rocket's red glare, the bombs bursting in air,

★ **FAST FACTS** During the battle, British troops used a new kind of rocket. It was called a Congreve rocket. The rockets created bright red glares as they flew through the air.

Gave proof through the night that our flag was still there,

LOOK

How does the painting illustrate the lyrics?

★ **FAST FACTS** Congreve rockets were useful because they did not require a cannon to launch them. They could be set off from light-weight tubes. But they were not very successful against a **fortified** structure like Fort McHenry.

"It seemed as though mother earth had opened and was vomiting shot and shell in a sheet of fire and brimstone."

– Francis Scott Key, 1814

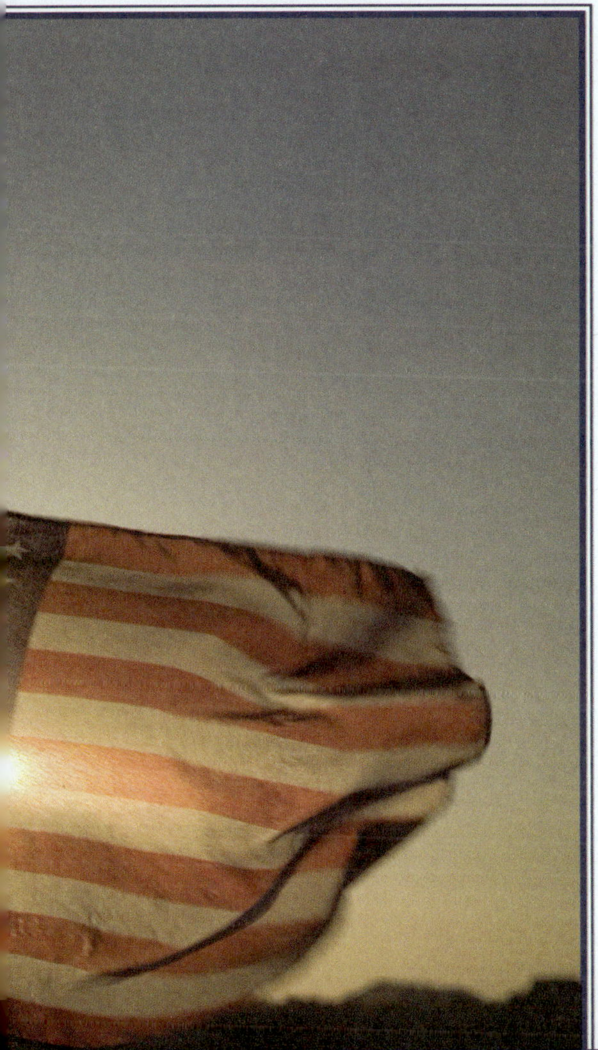

O say does that star-spangled banner yet wave
O'er the land of the free and the home of the brave?

★ **FAST FACTS** The term "star-spangled banner" became a nickname for the United States' flag. Today, the flag has 50 stars and 13 stripes. The last two stars were added in 1959 and 1960.

On the shore dimly seen through the mists of the deep

★ **FAST FACTS** Baltimore and its harbor sit on the Patapsco River where it empties into the Chesapeake Bay. As a **coastal** city, the wet sea air can cause fog.

*Where the foe's **haughty** host in dread silence **reposes**,*

CREATE

Make a list of unknown words in the song. Look up their meaning. Then rewrite the lyrics in your own words. Does the meaning change?

★ **FAST FACTS** Fort McHenry was guarded by 1,000 soldiers. The British admiral, Alexander Cochrane, commanded 5,000 troops during the attack on the fort. When the attack ended, four American soldiers had given their lives and 24 were wounded.

What is that which the breeze, o'er the towering steep,

★ **FAST FACTS** Forts like Fort McHenry are often built on higher ground. Steep mounds of earth were sometimes built up for protection. Fort McHenry's cannons were placed on top of mounds facing out towards the water.

As it fitfully blows, half conceals, half discloses?

THINK

Why do you think the song includes questions? Would the song be different without them? How so?

★ **FAST FACTS** Fort McHenry's large garrison flag was sewn by local flag maker, Mary Young Pickersgill, with the help of her daughter, her nieces, her mother, her apprentice, and more. A replica is flown at Fort McHenry today. The original is on display at the Smithsonian Institute.

★ **FAST FACTS** Besides the attack from the sea, other British forces were stopped on land heading towards Baltimore. While 1,000 soldiers defended the fort, 10,000 defended the road. Without taking the fort, the British troops could not take Baltimore.

Now it catches the gleam
of the morning's first beam,
In full glory reflected
now shines in the stream,

'Tis the star-spangled banner – O long may it wave

★ **FAST FACTS** The United States flag has been part of other important moments in history. In 1945, the flag was raised by U.S. Marines at Iwo Jima. In 1969, it was flown on the moon during the first moon landing.

O'er the land of the free and the home of the brave!

ASK QUESTIONS

What else do you want to know about the national anthem? Make a list of questions. Choose one and research the answer. What did you learn?

"Ours is the land of the free because it is the home of the brave. America's future will be great because our nation will be strong."

– President Ronald Reagan, 1984

TIMELINE OF AN ANTHEM

September 17, 1814	Francis Scott Key's poem "Defense of Fort McHenry" is printed with a suggestion of how it can be sung.
Late 1814	Thomas Carr prints and sells the song from his music store. He retitles it "The Star-Spangled Banner."
1889	"The Star-Spangled Banner" is made the official song to be played when raising the flag.
1916	President Woodrow Wilson makes it the official anthem of the U.S. Armed Forces.
1931	An act of Congress declares "The Star-Spangled Banner" the national anthem of the United States. President Herbert Hoover signs the act into law.

LEARN MORE

BOOKS

Harris, Beatrice. *Why Do We Have a National Anthem?* New York: Gareth Stevens, 2025.

Quinn, Jamie. Discover *"America the Beautiful": A Tribute to Our Nation*. Ann Arbor, MI: Cherry Lake Press, 2026.

Van Zee, Amy. *The War of 1812: Independence Secured*. Ann Arbor, MI: Cherry Lake Press, 2026.

WEBSITES

Search these online sources with an adult.

The National Anthem, The Star Spangled Banner | United States Marine Band via YouTube

Fort McHenry | National Park Service

GLOSSARY

coastal (KOH-stuhl) describing where land and sea meet

detained (dih-TAYND) held in one place; stopped from leaving

garrison (GAIR-uh-suhn) a military post

haughty (HAW-tee) arrogant and prideful

negotiate (nih-GOH-shee-ayt) come to an agreement with another party

ramparts (RAM-parts) protective barriers used in defense

reposes (rih-POHS-uhz) rests after hardship; state of rests after death

siege (SEEJ) military attack

INDEX